From
to **Space**

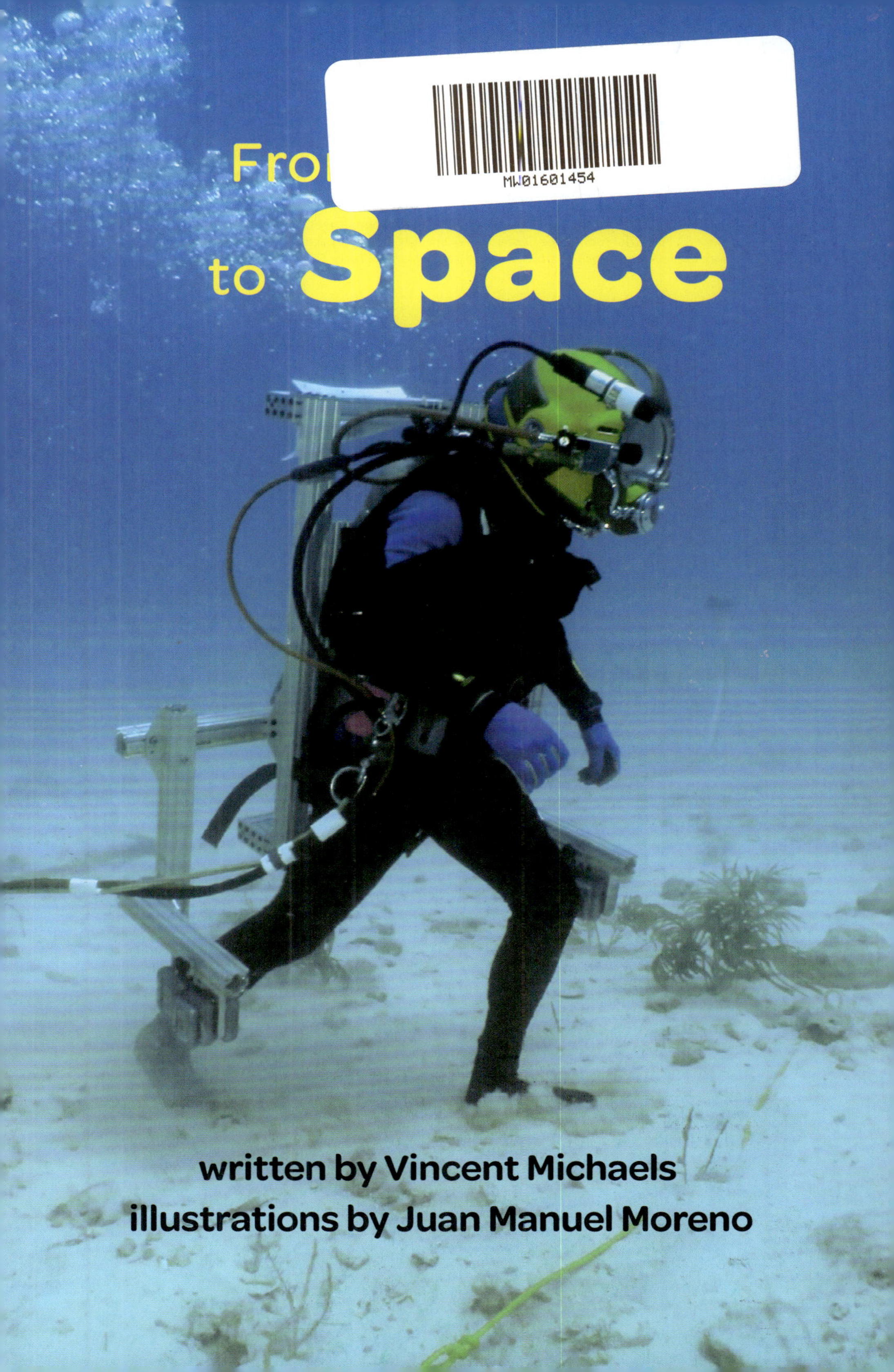

written by Vincent Michaels
illustrations by Juan Manuel Moreno

Contents

CHAPTER 1
Space and Sea

The word *astronaut* comes from Greek words that mean "star sailor." That is just what astronauts are. Their ships fly through space like it is the sea.

Space is a hard place to live and work. It is dark and cold and has no air or food.

2

Astronauts must train for space missions. But sending astronauts to space costs a lot. Getting ready takes a long time.

NASA is the U.S. agency in charge of air and space science and technology.

So, NASA trains astronauts here on Earth.

But where on Earth is extreme like space?

Under the sea! Being deep in the sea is a
lot like being in space. There is no air.
Your body must adjust to the new
place. You are far from home.
And you can't just leave when
you want to.

NASA came up with a smart plan to train astronauts for space. It would send them under the sea.

This is how Project NEEMO was born.

NASA also sends astronauts to other extreme places on Earth, including deserts, volcanoes, and icy regions near the North and South Poles.

CHAPTER 2

Project NEEMO

Project NEEMO started in 2001. NEEMO sends teams of astronauts under the sea to train for space. They become aquanauts, or people who live and work underwater.

NEEMO stands for "NASA Extreme Environment Mission Operations."

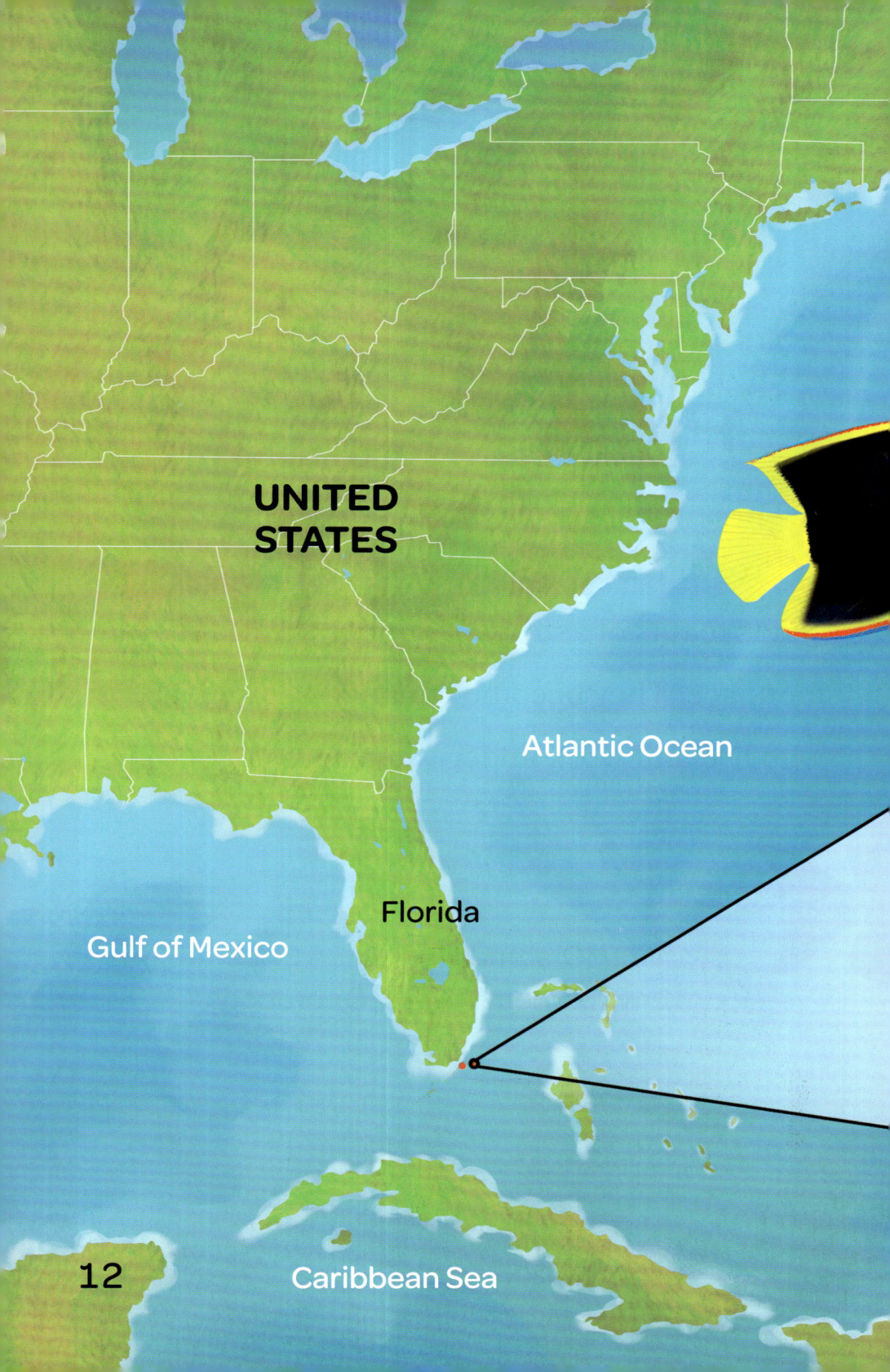

UNITED
STATES

Atlantic Ocean

Florida

Gulf of Mexico

Caribbean Sea

NEEMO crews train at Aquarius. This base is near coral reefs off the coast of Florida. It is 62 feet below the surface. That's deeper than a bowling lane is long!

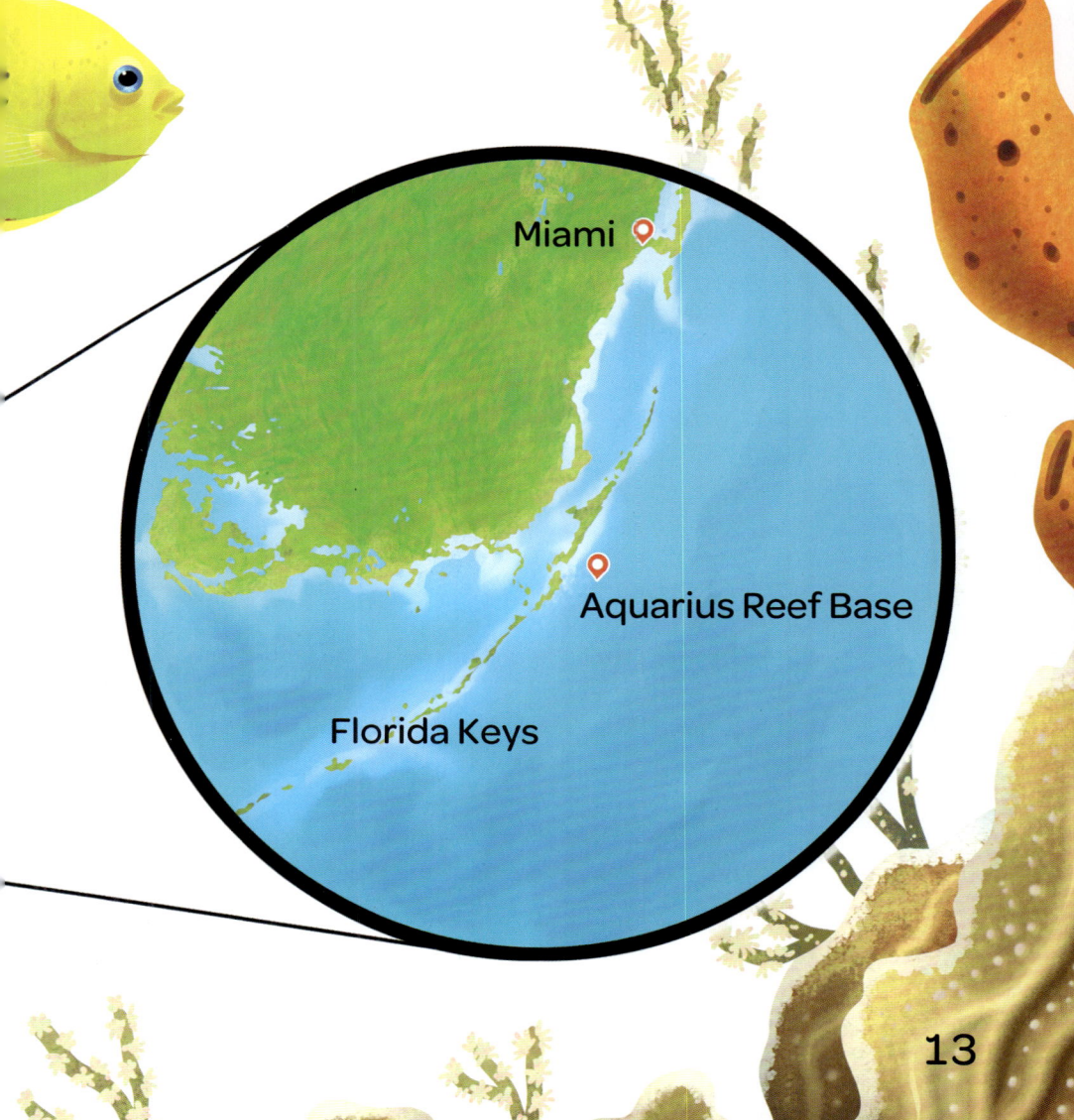

Miami

Aquarius Reef Base

Florida Keys

Air, power, and communications come from the life support buoy that floats on the surface.

Aquarius stands on a 120-ton platform that keeps the base from floating. Long cords connect it to fresh air and power. These cords also let the crew talk to people on land.

The base is 43 feet long and 9 feet wide. That's about the size of a school bus. But unlike a bus, the base can hold just 6 people at a time.

Most NEEMO crews have 4 astronauts. They work with 2 people who run the base. More team members help from dry land. A mission can last up to 3 weeks.

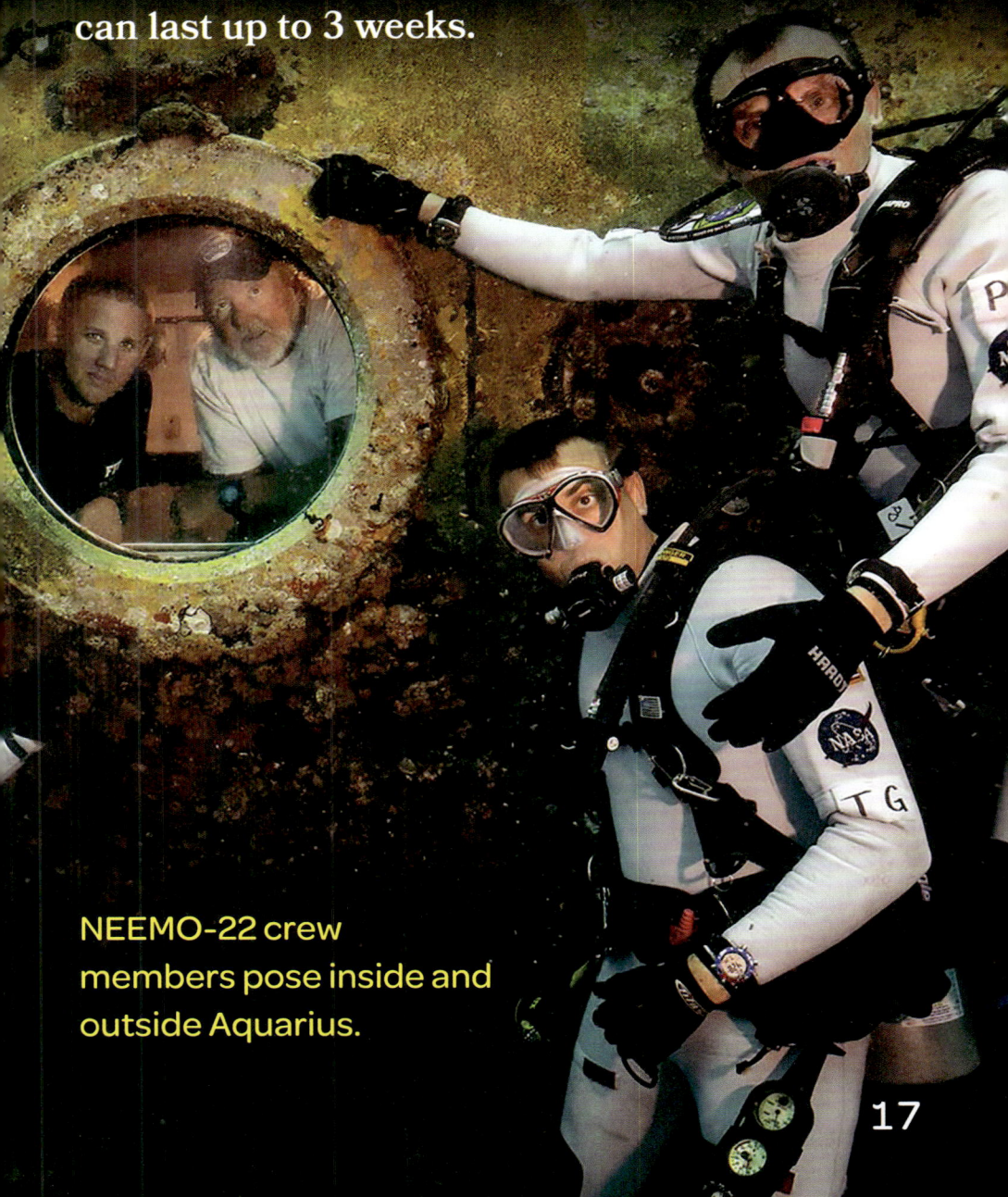

NEEMO-22 crew members pose inside and outside Aquarius.

CHAPTER 3
Welcome to Aquarius

There is just one way to get to Aquarius. Swim! The crew put on wet suits. They add masks, fins, and air tanks. Then the crew dive down to the base.

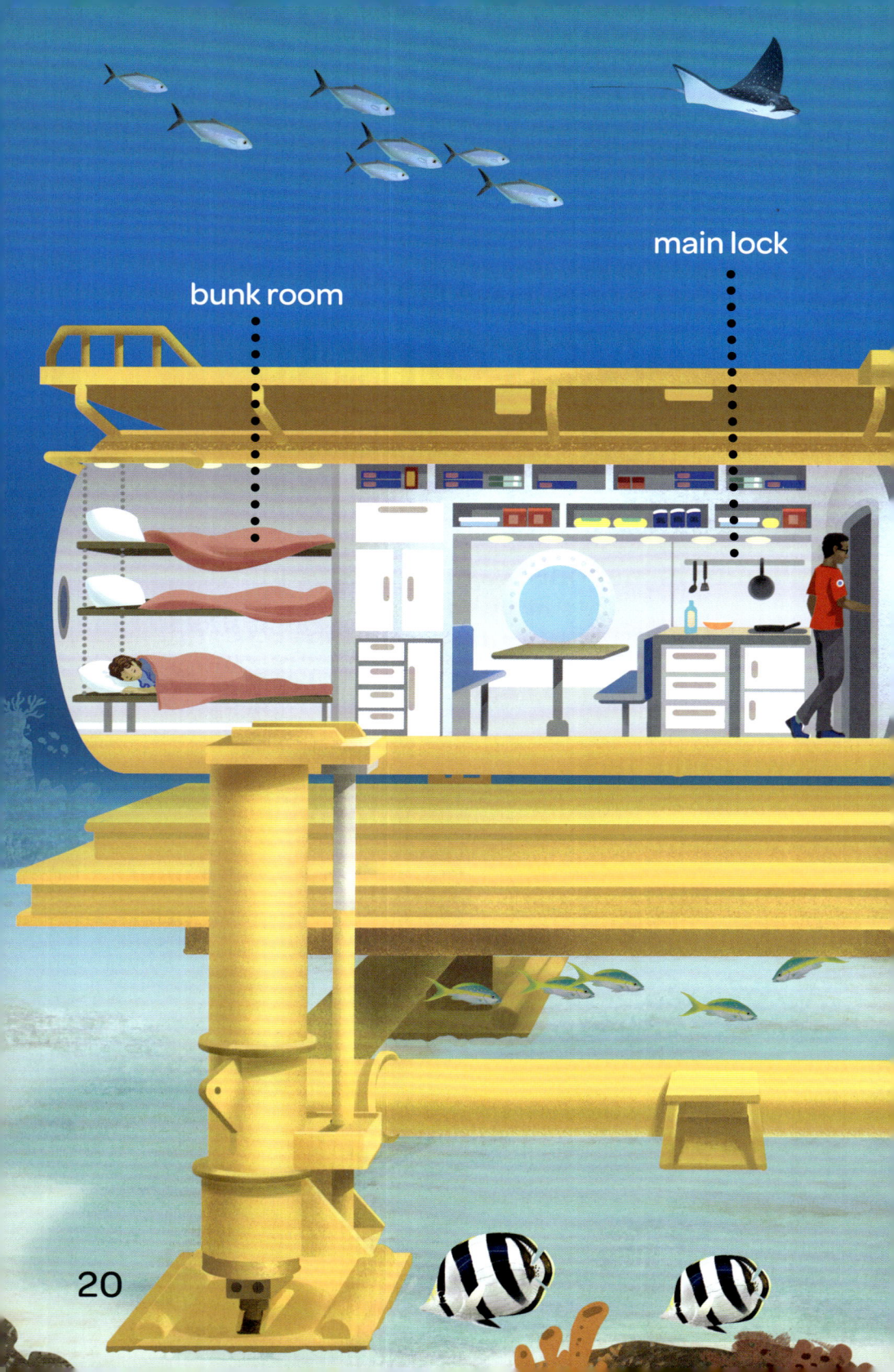

bunk room

main lock

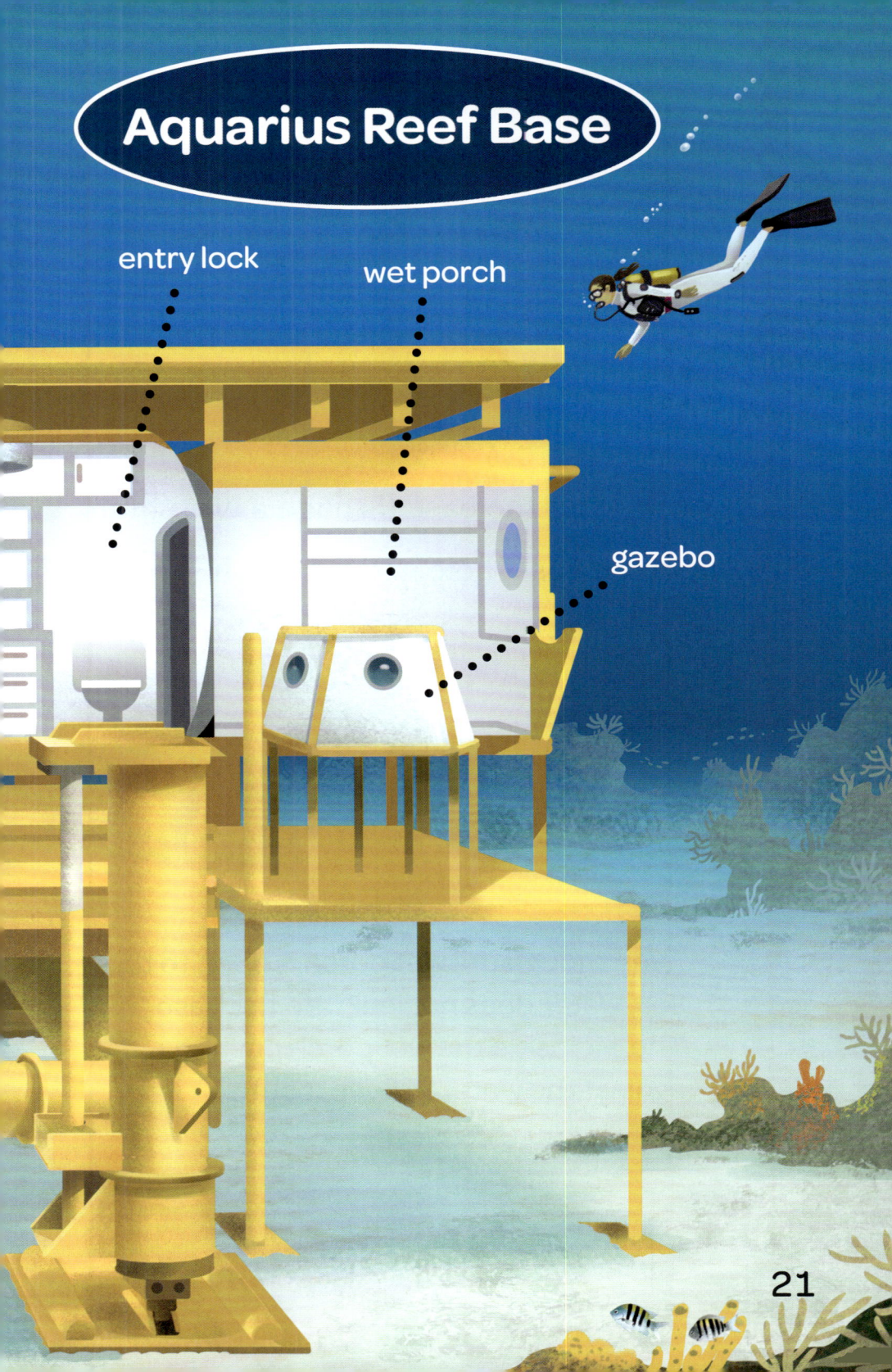

Aquarius Reef Base

entry lock

wet porch

gazebo

The crew enter the base through a wet porch. This tiny room has a hole in the floor! It is open to the sea.

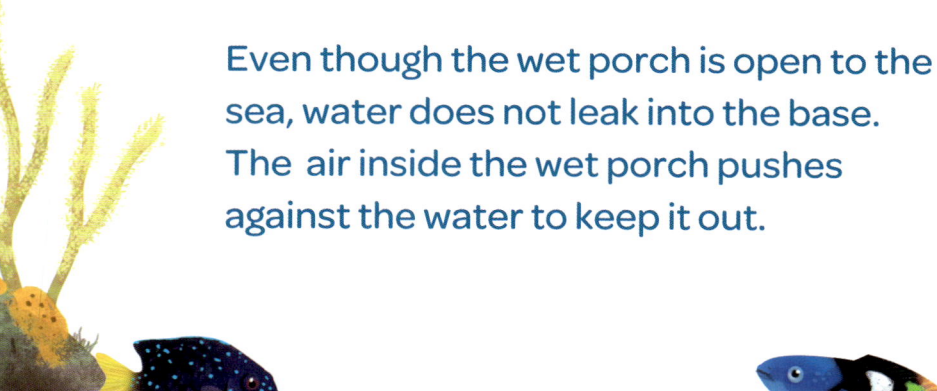

Even though the wet porch is open to the sea, water does not leak into the base. The air inside the wet porch pushes against the water to keep it out.

The crew shed their gear and cross into an entry lock. This small room contains a lab. Here, the crew can work and conduct tests. Next to the lab is a bathroom.

The entry lock connects to the main lock. The crew spend most of their time here. The kitchen has a sink, fridge, and microwave. The crew can make quick meals. They add hot water to freeze-dried food. You might eat food like this when you go camping.

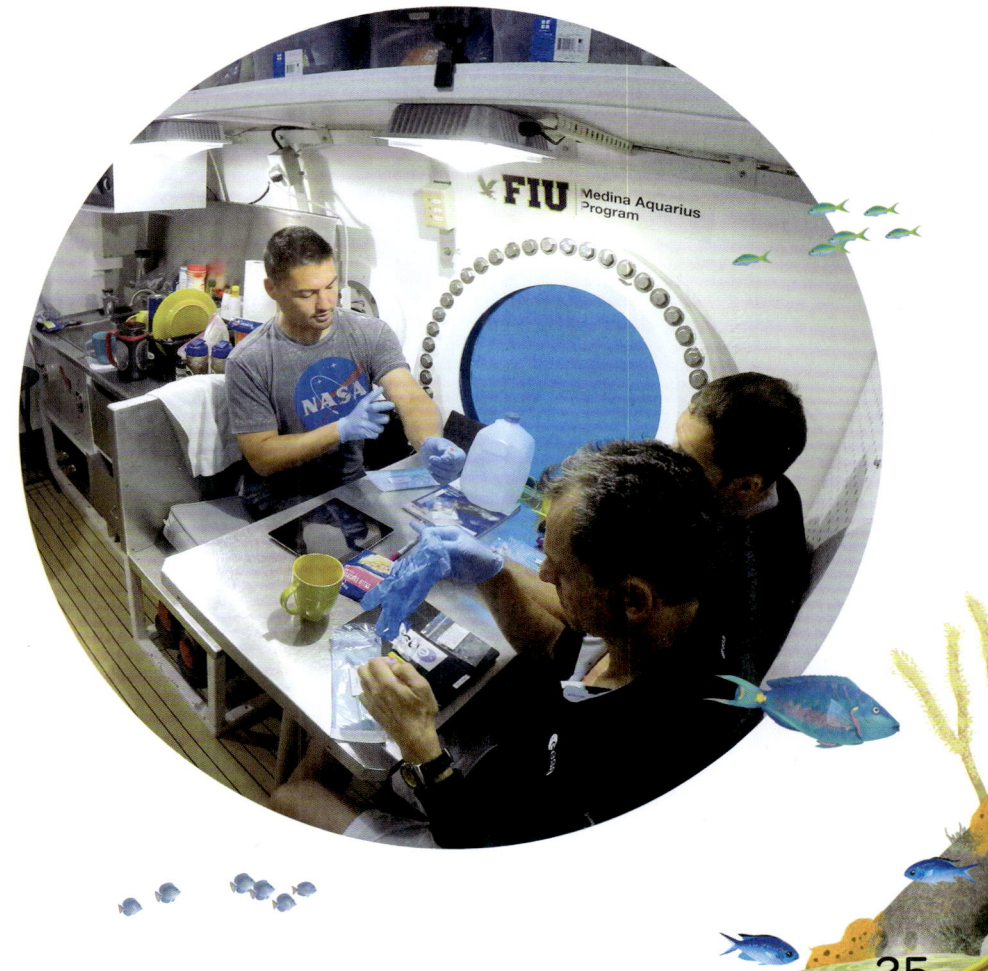

At the table, the crew eat, talk, and work. They also peer out a big glass window, or porthole. They see stingrays, eels, and other fish. The reef is home to more than 6,000 kinds of sea life!

The porthole is like the crew's very own aquarium!

Six bunkbeds are stacked at the far end of the base. As the crew rest, they can look through a smaller porthole.

The base also has a deck with a gazebo. This is where the crew can go if the power goes out. It holds a supply of air.

If something goes wrong, the crew must act fast. Any problem can put them in danger. Just like in space, they must work as a team. And just like in space, they are not alone. They can call crew members on land for advice.

CHAPTER 4
The Crew at Work

Like many spacecraft, Aquarius is small. The crew get used to living together in tight quarters. This closeness helps them prepare for long space missions.

Some crews become like a family. They help each other complete tasks. They fix problems as a team. They build trust. These are skills crews need in space.

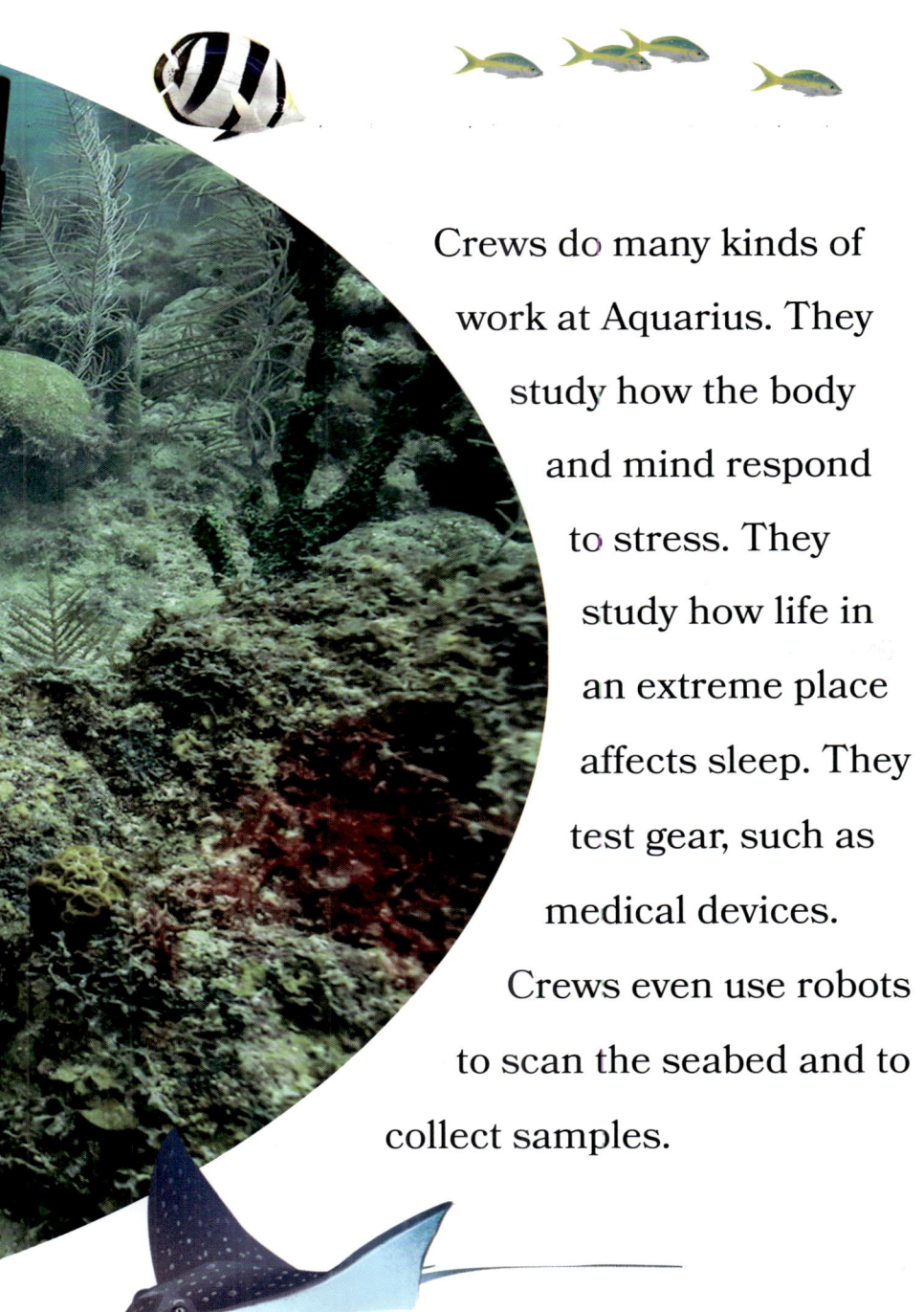

Crews do many kinds of work at Aquarius. They study how the body and mind respond to stress. They study how life in an extreme place affects sleep. They test gear, such as medical devices. Crews even use robots to scan the seabed and to collect samples.

Crews also do deep sea dives, which are a lot like spacewalks. These dives do not happen without a plan. Like a spacewalk, each dive has goals and a time limit. The crew will have many tasks in space. They may not have a lot of time. Training helps the crew learn to work quickly.

NEEMO-16 crew members explore the seafloor with a small underwater vehicle.

Sometimes the crew explore the reef. Sometimes they collect data about sea life. One NEEMO crew studied the size and health of coral. They made maps to show where coral was and was not growing well.

Aquarius is inside the Florida Keys National Marine Sanctuary. This special area protects one of the largest living barrier reefs in the world.

Other training tasks involve working as a team to build something. Some NEEMO crews have made underwater labs. One crew made "trees" out of plastic pipes. These trees help new coral grow, restoring the reef.

41

In space, astronauts feel like they are floating. Water makes people float, too. During dives, the crew can try out that feeling of floating. They can load up on gear to float less. They can remove it to float more. This way, the crew can feel what walking on the Moon or Mars might be like.

What does a moonwalk in a space suit feel like? Walking on the seafloor with this "backpack" gives this NEEMO-9 crew member a pretty good idea.

During long dives, the crew might stop at a way station. Way stations are like rest stops. They are set up around the base. Inside, the crew can take off their masks. They can talk, eat a snack, and refill their air tanks.

A member of NEEMO-13 takes a break inside a way station.

CHAPTER 5
Going Up

When their work is over, the crew prepare to leave. But getting back to the surface is not as easy as it seems.

Under the sea, water presses down on you. The deeper you go, the stronger that feeling gets. This is called pressure. You can feel it in your ears when you swim to the bottom of a pool.

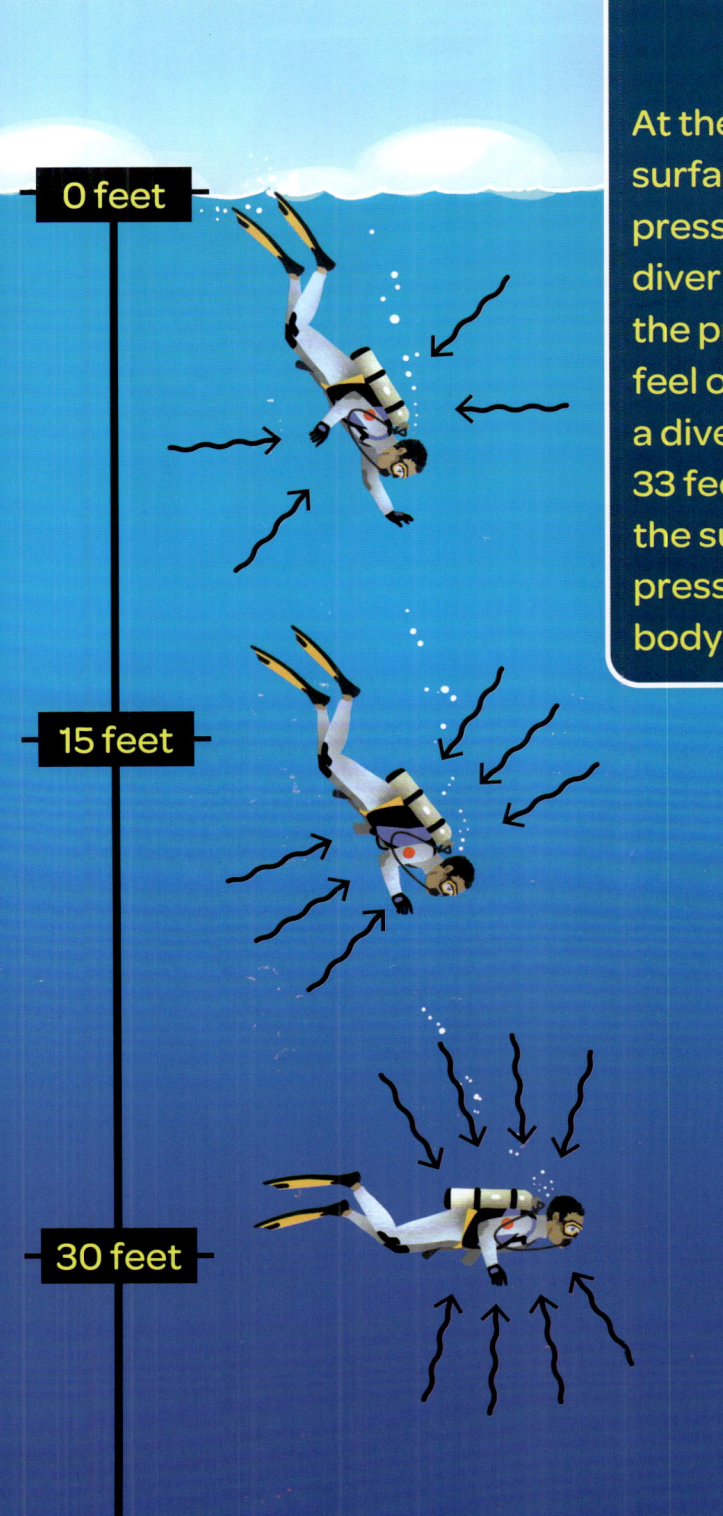

0 feet

15 feet

30 feet

At the ocean's surface, the pressure on a diver is similar to the pressure they feel on land. When a diver reaches 33 feet below the surface, the pressure on their body doubles.

Fast changes in pressure can be harmful to your body. The crew have spent a long time deep underwater. Their bodies need time to prepare for less pressure. That's why they can't just leave the base and swim up.

Instead, the crew rest while air is slowly pumped out of the base. Little by little, the pressure shifts. Little by little, their bodies adjust. After 16 to 18 hours, the crew can safely swim up.

While they rest and watch a movie, the NEEMO-10 crew wear oxygen masks. Breathing oxygen helps their bodies adjust to the pressure change before they swim up.

Back on land, the crew see blue sky for the first time in days. They know that hidden in the sunlight are stars and planets.

It is time to go home, but only for now. The crew members are no longer aquanauts. They are astronauts, "star sailors" ready to explore space.

John Herrington has been a Navy pilot, a test pilot, and a NASA astronaut. He is also a citizen of the Chickasaw Nation. He is considered the first citizen of a Native American tribe to fly in space.

Meet Commander John Herrington

In 2002, Herrington flew to the International Space Station (ISS). There, he went on three spacewalks. In 2004, he led NEEMO-6. His crew spent 10 days at Aquarius. We asked him about those trips.

Question: A lot of people go under the sea to train for space. But you went to space first! How did that happen?

Answer: Well, NASA wanted to train a team that had never flown in space. I had already been to space, so I was the commander. Space is a strange place. It can be dangerous. A little bit scary. The sea is the same way. So we had a chance to go underwater and say to the newer astronauts, "Hey, this is what space is like. Except it is not wet."

Q: What is it like to live and work inside Aquarius? How did it compare to the International Space Station?

A: The ISS is much bigger. There is very little gravity in space. You can float and do your work anywhere, such as on the ceiling or the walls. On Aquarius, there is gravity. You have to stand on the floor while you work.

Q: What was a normal day like on your NEEMO mission?

A: We would get up and eat together. Then we would plan our "spacewalk." We had a checklist and a timeline, just like in space. We would dive and then have lunch. Sometimes people swam down to drop off supplies. Sometimes we did experiments. At night, we read or talked. The lights made fish come check us out. They would swim outside the windows and look in!

Q: Did anything funny or scary happen?

A: One time, Doug Wheelock and I dove to a deep way station. It was about 100 feet down. We filled our tanks and talked to the base. Doug left first. I put my mask on and dove out. Then I saw Doug. His eyes were so big. He pointed, and I turned around. A big manta ray was swimming right at us. It was doing a big, huge swoop with its fins. Its mouth was massive. You do not see that in space!

Q: What advice do you have for kids who want to be astronauts?

A: I would say, "Do a job you love." If you want to be an astronaut, you have to go to school for many years. Then you have to get a job and learn to work well with others. After that you can apply to be an astronaut. If you are chosen, great! But not everyone gets chosen. If you do a job you love, you will be happy either way.

More

Three, two, one . . . liftoff! Many aquanauts train underwater to prepare for life above Earth as astronauts. Some astronauts travel to the International Space Station (ISS). The ISS orbits 250 miles above Earth's surface.

Astronauts from all over the world live and work aboard the ISS. The station is as big as a football field. It has six sleeping areas, two bathrooms, and a gym. While aboard, astronauts perform experiments in a laboratory. They have learned how to grow plants in outer space. They have even learned how to use lasers to communicate with people on Earth.

Did you know that people have been living in space since the year 2000? More than 270 astronauts have called the ISS "home," including John Herrington. Commander Herrington even performed three spacewalks to help build the station. He called the mission "the high point of my working life."

Do you want to see the ISS from your backyard? A NASA website shows how and when to spot the station. It is the third brightest object in the night sky. The ISS moves even faster than an airplane! Look up when it passes over your neighborhood to catch a glimpse.